OLDE-TIME HEARTLAND

KITCHEN HINTS & TIPS

Michele Price Mann

Publications International, Ltd.

Michele Mann is a freelance writer who lives with her husband and four kids in a beautiful stretch of country right outside Birmingham, Alabama. A city girl at heart, she is adapting to life in the wide-open spaces and learning how to slow down and enjoy the simple things.

Cover Illustration: Steve Noble

Interior Illustrations: Art Explosion, Jupiterimages, Shutterstock

Louis Weber, CEO
Publications International, Ltd.
7373 North Cicero Avenue
Lincolnwood, Illinois 60712

ISBN-13: 978-1-4508-0903-0

ISBN-10: 1-4508-0903-0

Manufactured in China.

8 7 6 5 4 3 2 1

Contents

THE HEARTLAND KITCHEN REBORN

Sometimes it seems that, despite our modern conveniences, we actually have less time for the people and things we care most about. The race to get new-fangled gadgets has become a distraction from what's most important in life—home, family, community. And the kitchen, the traditional heart of the home, has become simply a quick pit stop in our dash to keep up with the Joneses. It's no wonder we pine for simpler, slower times.

If you long for a more home-centered path through daily life for yourself and your family, a good place to start is in the kitchen. Turning your kitchen into a place of commonsense cooking, good eating, and togetherness—a place for appreciating the simpler joys of life—is easier than you might think. In this little book, you'll discover many of the old-fashioned, practical, and thrifty ways of the traditional heartland kitchen. You'll learn how to stock your pantry and icebox with versatile basics and how to store your foods properly to help ensure freshness, flavor, and nutrition. You'll find handy heartland cooking and baking solutions, as well as tips for using common cooking supplies to make kitchen cleanup easier. You'll even discover simple, inexpensive ways to bring nature indoors and to create an inviting space for making and sharing meals and nurturing the ties that bind. This handy collection of heartland know-how can help you turn your kitchen back into the heart of your home.

STOCK THE RIGHT STUFF

Hearty, home-cooked meals, shared with loved ones around the kitchen table, have always been treasured mainstays of living in the heartland. But keeping that tradition alive amidst life's many demands hasn't always been easy. Fortunately, experienced heartland cooks have learned a valuable trick: Keep a well-stocked, wisely equipped kitchen. Having certain basic ingredients and tools always on hand enables even the busiest cooks to whip up hearty breakfasts or budget-friendly family dinners without hours of planning and preparation. To prime your kitchen for cooking, use the tried-and-true tips in this chapter.

Prepare Your Pantry

**Even the most resourceful housewife cannot
create miracles from a riceless pantry.**

—CHINESE PROVERB

If you were ever asked to fetch something from your grandmother's pantry, you probably remember it looking like a miniature country store. Its shelves likely heaved with home-canned fruits and vegetables, little tins and jars of seasonings, bags of cornmeal and rice, hefty canisters marked "Flour" and "Sugar," and more. Grandma stocked the dry goods and canned foods she could turn into tasty meals with little fuss (but lots of love). Follow her lead by filling your own pantry with these handy basics:

Pasta and Rice

Pasta and rice are like good friends—they're reliable, they get on well with your other food "friends," you can keep them a good long time, and you don't have to spend big bucks to acquire them. You'll want these pantry pals close, so they're there when you need them to satisfy heartland appetites large and small.

> ## Handy Hint
>
> Be sure to watch for sales on canned and frozen items, then stock up. But don't go overboard. Keep in mind how much food (and which kinds) your family will consume in, say, a month or six weeks and how much free space you have in your pantry and freezer.

Pasta. It's the perfect partner. Store a ready supply of old favorites, such as spaghetti and macaroni, for tossing with chopped vegetables; ground meat or leftover chicken; and/or your favorite sauce. Stock egg noodles, too: Boiled quickly and tossed with butter and grated cheese, they go great with beef or pork.

Ever-reliable rice. Like pasta, rice is a quick and easy foundation for all sorts of sides and entrées. Classic long-grain white rice cooks quickly (in 20 minutes or so) and serves up light and fluffy. Medium- and short-grain rice retain more moisture, making their grains stick together for fork-friendly mouthfuls. And while it requires more cooking time (about 40 minutes), brown rice has a wonderful chewy texture, nutty flavor, and healthy fiber content that helps you feel fuller longer.

Canned Goods

Whether store-bought or put up at home, canned foods are the backbone of the pantry. They can handle a long stay on the shelf (they were, after all, bomb-shelter staples in the 1950s). They're ready to serve in no time. They even come in versions that are lower in salt, sugar, or calories for family members on special diets. So count the following canned goods among your pantry essentials:

Pasta sauce. Store a few jars for days when you don't have time to make this versatile sauce from scratch. Just heat it up and toss it with pasta. Use smaller portions to moisten meatloaf or casseroles. You can even use this old standard to spice up that decidedly modern convenience food—the frozen pizza. Stir some extra herbs and dried pepper flakes into a little sauce, and add it to a boring frozen pizza for an extra kick of flavor.

Tomatoes. Keeping a variety of canned tomato products (see box on page 8) and tomato paste on hand puts all sorts of soup, side-dish, and entrée options within reach.

Tuna. Canned tuna is an indispensable and nutritious pantry staple. By adding a little salt, pepper, and mayo, you get classic tuna salad, which you can jazz up with diced celery, pickle relish, or minced green onions. An inexpensive source of protein, tuna adds nutritional heft to salads, sides such as mac and cheese, and casseroles.

Count on Canned Tomatoes

Canned tomatoes come in several varieties and should be a constant presence in your pantry. The tomatoes were picked when perfectly ripe and processed right away to preserve their flavor and freshness. So not only do canned tomatoes save you a lot of time in the kitchen, they also tend to taste and cook up much better than the often flavorless or mealy, out-of-season, hothouse tomatoes sold in super-markets. Here are some different varieties of canned tomatoes and suggestions for using them:

Whole: Most canned whole tomatoes are peeled and packed in tomato puree or tomato juice. Because they are the "meatiest," whole tomatoes tend to add considerable flavor and texture to pasta sauces and casseroles.

Diced: These are whole tomatoes that didn't survive processing intact, so they were simply chopped up into smaller chunks. They're packed in tomato juice and are great additions to soups and stews.

Crushed: These mashed up tomatoes are packed in tomato sauce or puree. They may even contain some of the skins, which add flavor. Use crushed tomatoes to fortify heavier dishes.

Stewed: These tomatoes are cooked and seasoned (with anything from garlic or chilies to sugar) before they're canned. They're good heated and served as a side dish to accompany chicken or fish.

Stock. Canned beef, chicken, and vegetable stocks are good, quick starters for soups and stews. You can also use them to add extra flavor to other common dishes. For example, substitute chicken stock for water the next time you cook white rice, or sauté vegetables in a little stock rather than in high-fat oil or butter.

Beans. Dried beans are inexpensive, versatile, and nutrient-packed, but they usually require hours of soaking before you can use them to prepare a meal. Fortunately, a lack of time doesn't mean you have to forego these little nutritional gems. Just stock your pantry shelves with a few canned varieties. (Red, white, and black beans are good choices to have on hand.)

Fruits and vegetables. You can't beat canned fruits and vegetables for convenience and versatility. Plus, there's something singularly uplifting about savoring the summer sweetness of fruits, such as peaches, in the dead of winter. And while canned produce may not supply quite the same levels of vitamins and minerals as fresh or frozen, they still pack plenty of nutrients.

When Canned Goods Go Bad

The United States Department of Agriculture (USDA) says that, if stored in a cool, dry place, canned foods that are highly acidic, such as tomatoes, fruit and fruit products (such as jams and jellies), and most "pickled" foods, should last approximately 18 months. Low-acid canned foods such as meats, fish, and vegetables can last two to five years. To avoid buying or consuming tainted foods, always reject or discard a canned item if its can is dented, leaking, or bulging; if liquid squirts from the can when you open it; or if the food inside has a bad smell. (For information on proper storage of canned foods, see the next chapter, "Store Supplies Wisely."

The Baker's Dozen

Homemade breads and sweets are timeless traditions in heartland homes. Storing the following ingredients will make it easier to fill your home with the aroma of fresh-baked cakes, quick breads, and pastries in a snap.

Flour. Keep a five-pound bag of all-purpose flour at the ready for most of your baking needs as well as for making gravy, thickening soups and stews, and dredging meat, fish, and poultry. To add a nutritional boost to baked goods, stock some whole wheat flour, too, and substitute it for up to half of the white flour in your recipes. Cake flour is best for producing light, delicate cakes and pastries.

Baking soda. This leavening agent causes batter to puff up. It also helps cookies and cakes brown nicely.

Baking powder. This leavening is typically made of baking soda, cream of tartar, and cornstarch. Remember: You can substitute baking powder for baking soda, but not vice-versa.

Cornstarch. A must-have in the heartland kitchen, cornstarch is used to thicken puddings and pie fillings, and it lends lightness to cookies and other baked goods.

Granulated sugar. With a stash of granulated sugar on hand, you're always prepared to satisfy a sweet tooth.

Brown sugar. Varying amounts of molasses are added to granulated sugar to create light or dark versions of brown sugar. Both add moisture, flavor, and color to baked goods.

Confectioner's sugar. This is granulated sugar ground into a fine powder and mixed with a bit of cornstarch. Use it to create smooth-textured frostings, glazes, and candies.

Cocoa powder. It's not only called for in a variety of chocolate desserts, it makes that comforting childhood favorite—hot cocoa.

Chocolate chips. Available in varieties such as milk, semisweet, and bittersweet, these morsels are good to have on hand if you have a cookie fan—or chocolate fiend—in the house.

Dried fruits and nuts. These mix-ins (pecans, almonds, cashews, and other nuts; raisins and dried apricots, cranberries, bananas, and the like; coconut; and even sunflower, pumpkin, and other seeds) can be used to add nutrients, crunch, and flavor to baked goods. They also make a

Dried Beans: The Untold Story

Dried beans often get a bad rap because they require more preparation (rinsing, soaking, and simmering) than canned beans. But while dried beans are not exactly a convenience food, traditional cooks know that they have some unbeatable benefits. They are less expensive than store-bought prepared beans and, in most cases, contain no salt or other preservatives. Consequently, you can season them just the way you like or need them. You can enjoy them on their own or with rice. Or you can use them to make chili or to fortify soups or salads (a heartland favorite is to serve them with a big hunk of homemade cornbread). Sealed bags of red beans, black beans, and white beans (such as great northern and navy) will also keep for a long time in your pantry.

healthy snack (in moderation) to serve to unexpected guests or to send in lunchboxes or backpacks.

Cornmeal. Whether you opt for white, yellow, or even blue cornmeal, you can use it to bake up those old-fashioned heartland favorites: cornbread and corn muffins. Cornmeal also lends great flavor and texture to cookies.

Flavored extracts. Pure vanilla and almond extracts are wonderful flavor enhancers for cakes, cookies, and pies. (Skip the imitation extracts, many of which impart an unpleasant bitter taste.)

Cooking spray. If you want cakes, muffins, and quick breads to come out of the pan in one piece, keep cooking spray in your cupboard and apply a light coating to bakeware before adding batter. Another option, in a pinch, is to pour a bit of vegetable oil on a paper towel and wipe the oil around the inside of the pan.

Other Pantry Essentials

✳ The tried-and-true, all-American condiment trio—ketchup, mustard, and mayonnaise—should be mainstays in your pantry. Add depth to this trio by stocking a sampling of Dijon, coarse-ground, and honey mustards along with plain yellow.

✳ Two other versatile, flavorful condiments that have gradually won space in traditional heartland kitchens are hot sauce and salsa. They're sure bets for spicing up dishes.

✳ A selection of oils will help ensure a smooth-running kitchen. With its mild taste, vegetable oil is a good choice for cooking and baking. Olive oil is great for sautéing vegetables, and it adds a lovely flavor to pastas and salad dressings. For even more variety, stock smaller bottles of sesame and walnut oils.

❋ Serving assorted pickles and pickle relishes will win over the hot dog and sausage fans in your household.

❋ Take advantage of vinegars. Red- and white-wine, balsamic, and apple-cider vinegars work well in salad dressings, marinades, and sauces. White distilled vinegar is a household workhorse

Seasoned Cooks' Seasoning Selections

Herbs and spices dress up a dish like nothing else. Their flavors can be bold, subtle, or somewhere in between, and just a pinch can take your cooking from bland to blow-you-away. Every pantry needs a good stash of flavor enhancers, but if you've been by your grocer's spice section recently, you've probably noticed that there are lots of choices out there. Standard seasonings in many a heartland kitchen include:

Allspice	Cumin	Paprika
Basil	Curry	Parsley
Bay leaves	Dill	Red-pepper flakes
Black pepper, peppercorns	Fennel	Rosemary
	Garlic powder	Saffron
Cayenne pepper	Ginger	Sage
Chili powder	Marjoram	Salt (table, kosher, and seasoned)
Cinnamon, cinnamon sticks	Mustard	
	Nutmeg	Thyme
Clove	Oregano	

with a wide range of uses, from removing stubborn onion and garlic odors from your hands and rinsing potentially harmful residues from fresh produce to clearing slow-running drains and giving your windows a streak-free shine.

✹ Stock your favorite fruit preserves for baking and cooking as well as for topping toast or ice cream. Use a touch of apricot jam or cherry preserves to baste chicken or turkey.

✹ Honey is a natural sugar substitute that's delicious in baked goods, hot tea, salad dressings, and cooked glazes.

✹ Peanut butter—that protein powerhouse—makes a great sandwich spread, but its versatility also makes it a perfect addition to anything from savory sauces to sweet treats.

✹ Cereal isn't just for breakfast. It's a nutritious snack eaten when dry. And oatmeal, that heartland classic, makes a hearty breakfast as well as a handy baking ingredient.

✹ Purchased or homemade breadcrumbs give crunch to fried foods, but they can also be used as a binder in meatloaf or sautéed and seasoned to top casseroles. Make your own by tearing dry (but not stale) bread into pieces, grinding them in a blender, and storing them in an airtight container.

✹ Canned soups are another multipurpose pantry staple. They make quick and filling meals on their own. And adding them to main- and side-dish recipes is a handy, inexpensive way to enhance flavor and moistness. Chances are, some of your tried-and-true recipes call for—or could benefit from—canned soup.

✳ Even if there isn't a leaf of lettuce in the house, bottled salad dressings can come in handy. Use them as marinades, in cold pasta dishes, or as dips for vegetables, pretzels, or chips.

✳ In addition to a selection of canned vegetables, no pantry would be complete without potatoes, sweet potatoes, onions, and garlic. They have a seemingly endless array of cooking uses. (See page 26 in the next chapter for information on proper storage of these kitchen must-haves.)

✳ Evaporated milk is simply concentrated milk. It's an excellent substitute for cream or whole milk in cooking and baking recipes. (Note: Don't confuse this product with sweetened condensed milk, which is used primarily in baking. Otherwise, you could wind up with really sweet mashed potatoes!)

✳ Stock crackers for your snackers. Crackers can also pinch-hit for breadcrumbs in casseroles, meatloaf, and meatballs.

Build an Inventive Icebox Inventory

Since I travel so much, it's always great to be home. There's nothing like getting to raid my own refrigerator at two in the morning.

—AMY GRANT

To make the most of the limited space in your refrigerator and freezer, try to stock ingredients that can play more than one role in the kitchen, and look for new and creative ways to use your usual icebox inhabitants.

In the Fridge

Milk. Whether you prefer whole, skim, or something in between, milk is more than a refreshing, nutrient-packed drink. It's a natural accompaniment to cereal, cookies, and coffee or tea. You can also use a milk soak to tenderize and flavor chicken and fish.

Eggs. You can beat the incredible egg—but you can't match its versatility. Use it from breakfast to dessert, in everything from omelets to your aunt's pound-cake recipe. But before buying a carton, inspect each egg for cracks or breakage, and check the "sell by" date. (Generally, eggs that are properly refrigerated will still be good for up to two weeks after the "sell by" date. But use the Handy Hint at right and your nose and eyes to help you judge for sure: If an egg smells or looks bad when you crack it open, toss it!)

> ## Handy Hint
>
> Let's say the "sell by" date on your egg carton has passed, but you really need that last egg for the dish you're making. To test if it's still good, put the uncracked egg into a bowl filled with at least four inches of water. If it sinks to the bottom, it's good; if it floats, it's a goner.

Butter. Keep this time-honored kitchen staple on hand, because for some things, such as topping hot popcorn or making most baked goods, there simply is no comparable substitute.

Plain yogurt. Plain yogurt can be used to make dips, as a substitute for sour cream in baking, and as a topping for baked potatoes. For a yummy, healthy breakfast, snack, or dessert, mix in your favorite fruit and even some nuts and/or granola, if you like.

Fruit juice. Orange, cranberry, apple—the choices are many, and they're not just for drinking. Juices can sweeten baked goods and enhance cooking sauces and marinades. Keep a pitcher of juice in the fridge, and stock the freezer with a couple tubes of frozen concentrate (try different flavors) that you can mix up as needed.

Cheese. Cheese comes in so many varieties and forms and has so many uses that it just makes good sense to keep some on hand. Stock a soft, spreadable variety (such as cream cheese or brie) to smear on crackers or bagels for a filling snack. And reserve cheese-drawer space for a hard cheese or two (cheddar and Swiss are popular) that you can slice and add to sandwiches or shred and sprinkle over salads, veggies, or soups.

Deli meat. Tuck it between bread slices for a portable meal, or roll it up and serve it with assorted cheeses and veggies for lunch or a light dinner or as impromptu appetizers when friends drop by.

Fresh fruit and vegetables. Let your tastes and the season help guide you in selecting produce to stock in your fridge. Even in the dead of winter, when many vegetables are out of season—which typically means they're harder to find, of poorer quality, and/or more expensive—at least stock your crisper drawer with fresh carrots and celery. Sliced and dipped in fat-free salad dressing, they make crunchy, satisfying snacks. When chopped, they go well with pot roast and make great additions to soups, stews, and stuffing.

In the Freezer

Meat (beef, poultry, pork, etc.) Stock up when your favorite cuts are on sale. To avoid playing the "mystery meat" game, wrap pieces well in freezer paper and label them with the type of meat, cut, and date frozen. Thaw them in the refrigerator, not at room temperature or in hot water.

Vegetables. Today, most varieties of frozen vegetables are flash frozen at the peak of freshness, which helps maintain crispness, color, flavor, and nutrients. So don't feel like you're short-changing your family by using them. Indeed, stocking frozen vegetables allows you to serve your family a healthy variety of vegetable dishes no matter the time of year. Just don't spoil a good thing. Choose a cooking method such as steaming or grilling that doesn't leach color and nutrients from produce or require added fat, go light on sauces or cheese toppings (they should complement, not cover, the flavor of the vegetables), and avoid overcooking (aim for crisp-tender).

Handy Hint

If you've ever discovered a mushy cucumber in the crisper drawer of your fridge or a layer of frost coating the ice cream in your freezer, you know how quickly foods can turn on you. One way to help ensure that your perishables survive and thrive is to avoid overstocking your cold spaces. Crowding your crisper or overpacking your freezer inhibits the circulation of cold air, which allows some areas and items to become too warm and others to get too cold. It also makes it easier for items to get lost and go bad before they're found again. (You'll find more icebox intel in the next chapter.)

Fruit. When fresh, in-season fruit isn't available at a reasonable price, you can still serve up blueberry pancakes, mix strawberries into your plain yogurt, or top angelfood cake with cherries if you keep frozen fruit on hand. The flash freezing that helps preserve vegetables likewise helps to lock in much of the flavor and nutritional value of fruit.

Bread. Freeze whole loaves or slices of white and wheat bread for

Spicing Up Your Meals

Perhaps you've thawed a roast, or your neighbor has just presented you with some of his freshly caught trout. Rather than relying on your usual recipe, you'd like to give it a new twist of flavor from your spice rack. The lists below will help you put together winning spice combinations (a total of three spices per dish is usually sufficient) for seasoning main-dish meats.

Pork: Cumin, curry, dill, fennel, garlic, rosemary, sage, thyme

Beef: Allspice, basil, bay leaf, chili powder, curry, garlic, oregano, thyme

Chicken: Basil, bay leaf, marjoram, oregano, rosemary, sage, thyme

Seafood: Basil, curry, dill, garlic, ginger, mustard, oregano, parsley, tarragon

morning-toast emergencies. Hamburger buns freeze well and also make great stand-ins for sandwich rolls. And freezing bread dough means you can bake up steaming, fresh bread in no time flat.

Stock. Frozen beef, chicken, and vegetable stocks and broths can quickly transform leftover meats and veggies into warming soups and stews. Try freezing stock in ice cube trays so you can defrost and use only as much as you need for a dish or meal.

Tools of the Trade

In department stores, so much kitchen equipment is bought indiscriminately by people who just come in for men's underwear.

—JULIA CHILD

❋ ❋ ❋

You can go into a fancy kitchen store and buy all manner of cooking tools—from a lemon zester to an egg slicer. What you will likely end up with, however, is a kitchen drawer overflowing with underused gadgets and an overused wallet short on cash. A more sensible option? Follow the lead of the frugal heartland cook, who spends far less money to equip her kitchen with a few sturdy essential tools that can handle pretty much any cooking chore. Her must-haves include:

Cast-iron skillet. Many experienced heartland cooks wouldn't want to live without this versatile tool. Its résumé of cooking abilities is virtually endless—from baking cornbread, frying an egg, and blackening fish to sautéing vegetables and searing steaks. About the only thing you can't do in it is boil water (water can cause it to rust). Cooked food slides out easily from a cast-iron skillet that's well-seasoned—meaning it has developed a natural, nonstick, black coating on its inner surface from years of being well used and well cared for. And a simple wipe with a damp paper towel is usually all that's required for cleanup (see page 56). Cast iron is highly durable, inexpensive, and suitable for stovetop or in-oven use. If possible, see if you can acquire a well-seasoned skillet from an elderly relative or friend who has taken good care of it. If you must buy a new one, however, it's simple to season it yourself as follows: First, remove all packaging and stickers. Then, while you preheat the oven to 350°F, use a paper towel to generously coat the inner surface with cooking oil. Place the pan in the oven for an hour or so, and it's ready to use. The seasoning, or nonstick coating, will build gradually as you use oil to cook in the pan, but you can speed the process by repeating the above seasoning technique often.

> ## Handy Hint
>
> Here's a great tip for simplifying your restocking trips to the supermarket: Take some time to plan a weekly menu. Then check to see what ingredients you have on hand, and jot down the specific items you need to buy. (Note any staples that are running low, as well.) Such prep work can save you money, time, and stress.

Knives. Good knives can turn cooking from a pain to a pleasure. You may have to spend a bit more on them, but consider them an investment that will do most of the work for you for years to come. The best basic knives to have on hand are:

* **Chef's knife.** You'll do most of your chopping and slicing with a good eight- to ten-inch-long chef's knife. It cuts easily through harder vegetables (carrots, winter squash, potatoes) and can even tackle a whole roasted chicken or beef roast. This knife is also indispensable for chopping garlic and onions.

* **Paring knife.** This little gem (from 2½ to 4 inches long) is great for peeling veggies, coring apples, and slicing soft fruits such as ripe peaches. A paring knife can also be used to mince fresh herbs and debone a chicken (just be sure you clean it in hot, soapy water after using it on raw meat, poultry, or fish).

✳ **Serrated knife.** Nothing slices through fresh bread or cakes as well as a serrated knife. It also cuts cleanly through juicy tomatoes and hot-from-the-oven lasagna. Use a sawing motion when wielding this knife.

Cutting board. Do your countertops a favor and invest in a couple of sturdy, large-size cutting boards—ideally, one for preparing meat, fish, and poultry and the other for everything else. Whether you opt for wood or plastic, be sure to disinfect the board with antibacterial dish soap and hot water after each use.

Grater. Handy for shredding hard cheeses or for shaving off a bit of lemon zest, a grater breaks down food like nothing else.

Pots and pans. You really don't need a special pot for each cooking task. The basic cookware listed here can fulfill an array of cooking and baking needs.

- Large cookie sheet

- 13-×9-inch baking dish

- One 3-quart and one-4 quart saucepan. The 3-quart pan is great for sauces; the 4-quart is best for soups, pasta, or rice.

- One 10- to 12-inch roasting pan. You can make your Sunday roast or a one-dish meal in this size roasting pan. Make sure it's suitable for use both in the oven and on the stove.

Slow cooker. No heartland kitchen would be complete without a slow cooker. You can fill it with rice and chicken in the morning and have a table-ready, home-cooked meal by dinnertime.

STORE SUPPLIES WISELY

One of the many benefits of modern refrigeration is that you no longer have to chase a chicken around the chopping block to get a fresh-tasting Sunday supper. But keeping foods at their freshest still requires some good old heartland smarts. Abiding by the simple, time-tested storage tips in this chapter will help you keep everything from dry goods to frozen foods fresher longer, which can prevent waste and stretch your food budget.

Control Your Shelves

Organizing is what you do before you do something, so that when you do it, it's not all mixed up.

—A. A. MILNE

Organizing and storing dry goods, canned foods, and other shelf-stable items properly is the best way to maximize their shelf life and minimize waste while increasing your efficiency in the kitchen. Here are some heartland hints to help you maintain the quality of pantry items and keep track of what supplies you have or need.

Leave them in the dark. The enemies of most shelf-stable foods are heat, humidity, and light. So store these supplies in a cool, dry, windowless closet or cupboard that is as far as possible from the stove and other heat-producing appliances.

Keep it under wraps. Once you open a bag or box of rice, pasta, dried beans, flour, sugar, or similar dry good, transfer any unused portion to an airtight container. It'll keep bugs out and freshness in. To reseal an opened bag of snack food, tightly fold the open end over on itself two or three times, and clip it closed with a clothespin.

Handy Hint

If you like stale bread, refrigerate that fresh loaf. But if you'd rather preserve bread's oven-fresh taste and texture, store it at room temperature. An old-fashioned bread box, placed away from heat sources, makes a perfect loaf lair.

Give everything a place. Organizing your pantry shelves makes it quick and easy to grab the ingredients you need, see at a glance when certain supplies are running low, and create an organized shopping list. It also makes it less likely an item will get pushed to a back corner to linger unused long past its expiration date. One simple but effective organization method is to group like products together—keep all baking items on the same shelf, for example, and separate canned fruit from canned vegetables.

Check dates. While some packaged foods can safely spend months or years in your pantry, others go bad far more quickly. And some items, such as bottled cooking oil, lose months of shelf life the moment they are opened. So if a pantry item is not stamped with a "use by" date, take the time to label it with the purchase date and the date you opened it. For an item that does have a "sell by" date, mark on the package the date you opened it. And do a quick inventory of your shelves once a month to get rid of anything outdated.

Keep Produce at Its Peak

**Vegetables are the food of the earth;
fruit seems more the food of the heavens.**

—SEPAL FELICIVANT

❈ ❈ ❈

❈ A crisper (or produce) drawer in your fridge is the best place to store most vegetables, but even this space can get a little too humid for them. To absorb excess moisture and keep it from wilting your vegetables, line the drawer with dry paper towels, and replace them when they get saturated.

> ### Handy Hint
>
> Slip a couple of bay leaves into a countertop bowl of ripening fruit to help keep fruit flies away.

❈ Berries, cherries, grapes, apricots, and figs also do best in a towel-lined icebox crisper, and fruits such as peaches, pears, plums, nectarines, kiwi, and avocado should be stored there after they've been ripened on a counter at room temperature.

❈ Keep your fruits in one crisper drawer and your vegetables in another to prevent both from going bad more quickly.

❈ Salad greens are notoriously quick to go brown or limp. To lengthen their lives, try this trick: Wash greens thoroughly, remove any wilted or brown leaves, and dry the remaining leaves well. Poke a few small holes in a plastic bag, line the bottom of the bag with paper towels, and place the greens on the towels in the bag. Seal the bag and store in the crisper. The greens should stay fresh three to five days.

❋ Wash produce (except salad greens) right before eating them, not before refrigerating them, or they'll rot more quickly.

❋ Refrigerating a garden-fresh tomato will mute its flavor. Keep ripe tomatoes at room temperature and out of direct sunlight, and eat or use them as soon as possible. Ripen greenish tomatoes on a windowsill.

❋ If you want your mushrooms to keep for more than a day, store them uncut in a paper bag on a shelf in the main section of the refrigerator. To clean them prior to use, simply wipe them with a damp paper towel; do not rinse or soak them.

❋ Citrus fruits, such as oranges, lemons, and limes, stop ripening when they're picked, but they can rot, so store them in the icebox to keep them at their juicy finest for up to three weeks.

❋ As soon as you get fresh corn home, refrigerate it—with the husk on—until you're ready to cook it (preferably that same day). Warm temperatures turn corn's natural sugar to starch.

❋ Store whole garlic, uncut dry onions, potatoes, and sweet potatoes in the cool, dry, (and preferably well-ventilated) darkness of your pantry. But keep the potatoes and onions apart, or the spuds will go bad more quickly. The potatoes should be good for two months or so; the onions and garlic will last a while longer.

❋ Never store apples and bananas together, because they'll both rot prematurely. Separate them from other ripe fruit, too.

❋ One bad apple really can spoil the whole batch, so check for and remove any that have begun to show signs of rotting. If you'll be eating the remaining apples within the next week, you can keep them on the countertop. If you want them to last longer, though, stick them in the icebox, away from other produce.

> ## Handy Hint
>
> You can't beat locally grown fruits and vegetables for freshness and flavor. But you probably also can't grow all of your own produce. To fill in the gaps, head on over to a farmers market. Farmers markets typically offer all sorts of fresh (and often organically grown) produce. And buying from them helps keep smaller local farms in business. For more information about farmers markets and directions to any in your area, visit www.localharvest.org.

❋ Let your nose tell you where to store pit fruits, such as peaches and plums. If they smell heavenly, they're ripe and ready to eat. To preserve that sweet goodness for up to three days, stow the ripe fruit in the fridge. If they haven't yet developed that fresh, fruity aroma, put them in a paper bag on the counter to ripen them. To speed ripening, add an apple to the bag, but check the fruit for ripeness frequently, so they don't get mushy.

Manage Your Meats, Poultry, and Fish

Vegetables are interesting but lack a sense of purpose when unaccompanied by a good cut of meat.

—FRAN LEBOWITZ

It's cheaper to put meat on the family table if you can stock up during sales and take advantage of bulk pricing. To keep your inventory of meat flavorful and safe in your freezer for a good long while, though, you need to store it properly.

Ground meats. Ground beef, pork, veal, and lamb (as well as ground turkey) will keep in the freezer for up to three to four months if you leave them in their grocery-store packaging and add an outer layer of aluminum foil.

Steaks, chops, chicken breasts, and roasts. Steaks will keep for 6 to 12 months, chops for 4 to 6 months, chicken breasts for 9 months, and roasts for 4 to 12 months if you wrap them individually in plastic wrap and give each an outer jacket of aluminum foil. Wrapping each one separately also allows you to defrost only as many as you need for a meal.

Bacon and sausage. Bacon and sausage will keep well in the freezer for a month if you leave them in their original packaging and overwrap them with aluminum foil.

Money-Saving Fridge Maintenance

You can generate more green for your wallet by taking these simple steps to make your refrigerator work more efficiently:

- Make sure your fridge is located out of direct sunlight and away from heat sources, such as ovens, dishwashers, and heating vents.

- Position it slightly away from the wall or cabinets so air can flow freely over the coils.

- Every few months, vacuum the refrigerator coils and clean the areas around and beneath the appliance.

- Keep the refrigerator between 35 and 38 degrees Fahrenheit and the freezer compartment between 0 and 5 degrees Fahrenheit.

- Keep your refrigerator and freezer compartments full but not over-stuffed. Packing in too much prevents good circulation of cold air. Leaving it nearly empty forces it to work harder, especially after you open the door. If either compartment is close to empty, put some water-filled jugs or containers in it.

Whole chicken. If frozen in its original packaging, a whole chicken will keep for a whole year.

Fish. Here's a fish-freezing trick: Dip your fish in cold water, and place it on a cookie sheet in the freezer so it develops a coating of ice. Repeat the process until the coating is about a quarter-inch thick. Then seal the ice-coated fish in a reclosable plastic bag, and store it in the freezer. This technique works best for lean fish (including tilapia, cod, and haddock). Fattier fish, such as salmon, can be frozen this way, too. (The fattiest fish, such as herring and mackerel, don't freeze well at all.) Lean fish frozen this way will keep for six months; fattier fish will keep two to three months.

When stowing your meat purchases in the freezer, don't forget to label the outside wrapping of each piece with the date of purchase.

Use Care with Dairy and Eggs

Parties who want milk should not seat themselves on a stool in the middle of the field in hope that the cow will back up to them.

—ELBERT HUBBARD

Dairy products and eggs can spoil rather easily if not stored properly. The following tips will help keep them safe and fresh-tasting.

* While most dairy products do best on the cold main shelves of the icebox, cheese prefers a slightly warmer environment. So if your fridge doesn't have a cheese drawer, keep the cheese in a resealable plastic bag in the produce crisper.

* If you get a good deal on butter and don't need it all right away, store the excess in the freezer. This is especially important for unsalted butter, which doesn't keep as long as the salted variety.

* Dairy products and eggs are like sponges—they absorb the aromas and flavors of other foods in your fridge. So keep a tight lid on milk, sour cream, yogurt, and other dairy products, and store eggs in their original carton rather than in the open egg

tray commonly found in fridges. Set an open box of baking soda in the fridge to help neutralize potent food odors, and replace it every three months.

Know Thy Fridge

Not all spaces in your refrigerator are made equal. The main shelved area is typically the coldest. The drawers for produce, cheese, and/or lunch meat are a bit warmer. And the shelves or bins in the door are warmer still. So put dairy, eggs, and other foods that need consistent cold on the main shelves; store fruits, vegetables, cheese, and cold cuts in their respective drawers; and relegate condiments, salad dressings, and other often-used, less perishable products to the door.

Mind Your Leftovers

**The most remarkable thing about my mother is that
for thirty years she served the family nothing but leftovers.
The original meal has never been found.**

—CALVIN TRILLIN

❉ ❣ ❉

Leftovers can be great budget-stretchers—if you store them safely.

Cool them quickly. Get leftovers into the icebox as soon as possible, because food left out at room temperature for more than two hours can harbor bacteria that can make you sick.

Seal in quality. Store leftovers in containers with airtight seals to help them retain their flavor, texture, and color as long as possible.

Store small. Transfer leftovers into small, flat containers; they allow the food to cool more quickly, helping to prevent the growth of potentially harmful bacteria.

Save the date. Keep track of the time your leftovers spend in the fridge. Most foods safely keep for three to five days, at most.

Save Seasonings Correctly

Tomatoes and oregano make it Italian; wine and tarragon make it French. Sour cream makes it Russian; lemon and cinnamon make it Greek. Soy sauce makes it Chinese; garlic makes it good.

—ALICE MAY BROCK

❄ ❄ ❄

Experienced heartland cooks know the value of herbs and spices for enhancing all sorts of dishes—and the importance of storing those seasonings properly to preserve their unique flavors.

For dry herbs and spices:

❄ Don't store clear bottles of herbs and spices in a rack on the wall or on an open shelf or ledge above the stove. These displays may look impressive, but dried herbs and spices can quickly lose flavor, color, and quality when left exposed to heat, light, humidity, or air. They'll retain their culinary qualities longer if you keep them in airtight containers or resealable plastic bags in a cool, dry drawer or closed cupboard.

❄ Label seasoning containers with the date of purchase so you know when it's time to replace them. Properly stored, dried herbs and ground spices should last six months. Whole spices (like peppercorns or cinnamon sticks) will last one to two years.

For fresh herbs:

- For leafier herbs such as basil, parsley, or cilantro, trim the ends, and prop in a jar or glass with about an inch of water—much like you would fresh flowers. They will last about a week.
- For bushy herbs including rosemary, thyme, or chives, loosely wrap in plastic wrap or a paper towel and put in a cool, dry location, such as a crisper drawer or door shelf in your fridge. Moisture causes mold to form on these herbs, so keep them as dry as possible. They will last about a week if stored properly.

Lessons from the Past: Revisiting the Root Cellar

Back when families grew all their own vegetables, homes weren't the climate-controlled shelters they are today. To help extend the life of their produce, these inventive folks used root cellars. A root cellar was essentially a small, dark, protected space dug out of the cool earth close to the main house. There they kept root vegetables, such as potatoes, carrots, and turnips. In colder months, the root cellar sheltered winter squash, salted meats, and even some dairy items, keeping them cold but not frozen. Many modern-day, heartland gardeners are rediscovering the inexpensive practicality of the root cellar and are creating basement nooks to store the fruits of their own garden labors.

COOK WITH HEARTLAND KNOW-HOW

Heartland moms always seem to know how to do what needs to be done in the kitchen. Much of their cooking and baking wisdom was likely passed down to them by their mothers (and aunts and grandmothers), although they surely discovered a few tricks of their own along the way. So it just makes good sense to take advantage of that time-tested heartland know-how instead of trying to reinvent the rolling pin every time you cook.

Start at Square One

**In the childhood memories of every good cook,
there's a large kitchen, a warm stove,
a simmering pot, and a mom.**

—BARBARA COSTIKYAN

Moms and other good cooks in the heartland know from experience that going through a few simple prep steps before cracking a single egg can help ensure the success of a dish. Whenever you set out to make a recipe, start from square one by running through the following to-do list:

Choose carefully. If you're in a hurry, select a quick and easy recipe that has few ingredients. This sounds like plain old common sense, but sometimes when you have your heart set on making a certain dish, you can overlook how much time is truly required to prepare it. If you try to rush through a recipe that has complicated steps and a long list of ingredients, you're likely to be disappointed with the result. Save that masterpiece for a day when you can give it the time and attention it deserves.

Read through the entire recipe. Read the recipe top to bottom before you begin any preparations. Make sure you know how to perform each step, and confirm that the yield listed will result in at least the minimum number of servings you need without over-whelming your icebox with leftovers. (This is also the point at which you should calculate—and jot down—changes in ingredient amounts if you do need fewer or more servings. Keep in mind that getting such adjustments right can take some trial and error.)

Do an ingredient inventory. Go through the ingredient list, and confirm you have enough of each item on hand before you begin.

Check your tools. Just as you do for ingredients, review the recipe to ensure you have all the necessary utensils and equipment (or can perform the steps with supplies you do have). Actually dig out the items you'll need, so you're not in the thick of cooking or baking when you remember

Handy Hint

Misplaced your rolling pin or lent it to your daughter-in-law? No problem. Grab a can of tomatoes or beans from the pantry, cover the dough with waxed paper, and start rolling. An empty wine bottle and waxed paper will also work in a pinch.

you lent your mixer to your sister or discover your son borrowed your meat mallet to pound in tent stakes.

Lay it all out. Gather all of the supplies, and measure out the specified amount of each ingredient into its own bowl or cup.

Improvise Ingredients in a Pinch

I feel a recipe is only a theme, which an intelligent cook can play each time with a variation.

—MADAM BENOIT

Sometimes you simply don't get the benefit of time to gather and measure your supplies before you begin cooking or baking (sometimes you find out only an hour before a Scouts meeting that you were volunteered to make the treats). If you realize in the middle of a recipe that you're missing an ingredient, don't panic. Check the sensible substitutions that follow for a way to improvise a solution.

* In place of 1 teaspoon baking powder, use ½ teaspoon cream of tartar and ¼ teaspoon baking soda.

* As a substitute for 1 cup brown sugar, mix 1 cup white sugar and 2 tablespoons molasses.

* If your recipe calls for ½ cup salted butter but you only have the unsalted variety, add ¼ teaspoon salt to every ½ cup of the unsalted butter.

Vegetables Reborn

Don't get discouraged if you're in need of vegetables but find the ones you have are a bit past their prime. The following hints can help perk up veggies that have seen better days.

- Dunk droopy carrots and celery in a cold-water bath mixed with a teaspoon of sugar, then put them in the refrigerator for an hour or two.

- Bring wilted salad greens back to life with a brief soak in a mixture of cold water and lemon juice.

- Onions that have been lingering at the bottom of your vegetable bin for a while can become more "potent." To keep their more robust flavor from overwhelming your recipe, slice the onion and soak it in a cold-water bath for 10 to 15 minutes before adding it to your dish.

✳ If you need 1 cup buttermilk, try using 1 cup regular milk to which you've added 1 teaspoon lemon juice.

✳ Three tablespoons semisweet chocolate chips can take the place of one ounce semisweet chocolate.

✳ Three tablespoons unsweetened cocoa powder and one tablespoon butter can be used instead of one ounce unsweetened chocolate.

✳ If you need 1 cup dark corn syrup but only have the light variety, take ¾ cup light corn syrup and add ¼ cup molasses. (If the color of the final product doesn't matter, though, you can simply use 1 cup light corn syrup in place of 1 cup dark—or vice versa.)

❋ If you need 1 cup light corn syrup and have no corn syrup of any kind, mix 1¼ cups sugar into ¼ cup water, then boil the mixture.

❋ If a recipe calls for 1 tablespoon cornstarch, you can substitute 2 tablespoons all-purpose flour instead.

❋ If you only keep skim milk in the house but your recipe calls for 1 cup whole milk, use 1 cup skim milk to which you've added 2 tablespoons melted butter.

❋ As a substitute for 1 cup butter, you can use ⅞ cup vegetable oil or 1 cup shortening.

❋ As long as you don't need it for whipping, you can replace 1 cup heavy whipping cream with ⅔ cup whole milk mixed with ⅓ cup melted unsalted butter.

❋ For a recipe that requires 1 cup mayonnaise, you can add 1 cup whole sour cream or plain yogurt instead.

❋ For cooking or baking, use ¾ cup plain yogurt and ⅓ cup melted butter in place of 1 cup sour cream. For topping baked potatoes, chili, and tacos, use a tablespoon or so of fat-free plain yogurt in place of sour cream for a healthier side dish.

❋ You can substitute ½ teaspoon white vinegar or cider vinegar for 1 teaspoon lemon juice.

❋ Use ⅓ cup lemon juice in place of ¼ cup white vinegar.

❋ While fresh vegetables are best, in a pinch you can use ½ teaspoon onion powder in place of a small, chopped onion.

✳ Likewise, if you don't have any garlic in the pantry, you can use ½ teaspoon garlic salt or ⅛ teaspoon garlic powder in place of 1 garlic clove.

✳ If you're missing the cup of ketchup called for in your recipe, make do with 1 cup tomato sauce (jarred or canned), 4 tablespoons sugar, and 2 tablespoons white vinegar.

✳ If you need 1 cup beef or chicken broth, you can use 1 bouillon cube dissolved in 1 cup water instead.

✳ If your dish requires 2 cups self-rising flour but you only have regular flour, mix 2 cups regular flour with 1 teaspoon baking soda, 2 teaspoons baking powder, and 1 teaspoon salt.

✳ You can use 2 cups powdered sugar as a substitute for 1 cup granulated sugar.

Trust Traditional Stovetop Secrets

**The kitchen is a country in which there
are always discoveries to be made.**

—GRIMOD DE LA REYNIERE

Banish boil-over. Try this old trick to keep boiling water from spilling over onto the stovetop: Rub the pot's rim with butter or lard.

Make soup less salty. If your soup tastes too salty, add a chunk of raw potato. The spud will absorb some of the excess salt.

Let joe overpower odors. Cover up the smell of burnt food with the welcoming aroma of coffee by dropping a couple unbrewed coffee grounds on the hot stove.

Cook mash-perfect potatoes. Next time you make mashed potatoes, avoid the risk of overcooking the spuds by steaming instead of boiling them.

Say no to sticky pasta. Before you drain noodles, add a few drops of oil to prevent clumping.

Speed up your beans. A pinch of baking soda added to the cooking water will soften the tough outer skins of dry beans and decrease cooking time.

Bank on Old-Fashioned Bread Basics

The smell of good bread baking, like the sound of lightly flowing water, is indescribable in its evocation of innocence and delight.

—M.F.K. FISHER

❈ ❈ ❈

What's a heartland kitchen without a hot loaf of homemade bread or basket of freshly baked biscuits? Use these old-time bread-baking secrets to whip up your next batch of piping-hot country goodness.

❋ Making a good loaf of bread can be time consuming. Don't try to hurry the process by using rapid-rise yeast or self-rising flour.

You'll end up with a heavy loaf. Stick with regular yeast—and be patient.

❋ Use a large bowl to mix the ingredients for bread dough. It allows greater air circulation during the mixing process, which helps to produce a lighter, softer loaf.

❋ When making bread dough, add ½ cup flour at a time, and mix after each addition, to incorporate more air into the dough for a more tender loaf.

❋ Don't skimp on kneading—it allows gluten in the flour to be released and gives the bread a lighter texture.

❋ While kneading, avoid the temptation to add more flour to keep the dough from sticking. Just keep working the dough and it will soon start cooperating. Too much flour added at the kneading stage can result in a loaf that's too dense.

❋ The secret to making flaky biscuits is cutting in the butter, lard, or shortening (coating small bits of fat with flour and other dry ingredients) while it's very cold—even frozen—and working quickly, so the fat doesn't have a chance to melt.

Do You Have the "Hand?"

Back in the day, when a cook became an expert at making breads and piecrusts, folks said he or she had the "hand." It meant that the cook could tell by touch whether bread dough was kneaded enough for a perfect loaf or whether a piecrust would bake up light and flaky.

Use a pastry blender, a grater, a food processor set on pulse, two knives moving in a crisscross fashion, or even your fingers to cut in the cold butter or lard.

✳ Unlike yeast-bread dough, which requires kneading, biscuit dough should be handled only as much as needed to mix ingredients. Working it too much will result in biscuits that are more dense than delicious.

✳ To give biscuits an old-fashioned flavor and texture, bake them in a cast iron skillet. Butter the bottom of the skillet to avoid sticking, and place the biscuits less than an inch apart.

Learn Some Sweet Tricks

The dessert crowns the dinner. To create a fine dessert, one has to combine the skills of a confectioner, a decorator, a painter, an architect, an ice-cream manufacturer, a sculptor and a florist.

—EUGENE BRIFFAULT

Dessert is a sweet ending to any meal. To help ensure that your desserts and other baked goods bring smiles (and requests for seconds), give the following tricks a try.

✳ If a recipe calls for a stick of butter and also directs you to grease a cookie sheet or baking pan, use the smears of butter left on the butter wrapper to grease the bakeware. Simply rub the inside of the wrapper over the surface that needs greasing.

❋ The best way to soften butter for a cake or cookie recipe is to take it out of the icebox earlier that day and let it soften at room temperature. But if you forget or don't have time, try this: Use a cheese grater to grate the required amount of butter. It will come to room temperature in just minutes. (Microwaving is more likely to melt rather than simply soften the butter, and using melted butter in cake or cookie recipes will result in poor-quality baked goods.)

Energy-Wise Cooking

The following tips can help you save on energy costs.

- Baking in glass or ceramic allows you to set your oven temperature 25°F lower than if you're baking in a metal pan.

- Bake two dishes in the oven at once. If they require different temperatures, set the oven dial halfway between the two.

- Add salt to water to make it boil at a hotter temperature; it will cook your food more quickly.

- When heating a large pot of water to boiling, keep the lid on; the water will come to a boil more quickly.

❋ When using butter to make cookie or cake batter, be sure the mixing bowl is at room temperature; the same goes for the beaters, if needed. Using a hot-from-the-dishwasher bowl and/or beaters will melt the butter, which can ruin the batter.

❋ When creaming butter and sugar for a recipe, take your time. Properly mixing these ingredients together can help ensure the quality of your cookies and cakes.

Baking on Thin Air

If you've ever had to apologize for—or toss out—a batch of cookies with badly burned bottoms, you no doubt understand the importance of using a good-quality cookie sheet. Though it may cost a few pennies more, an insulated cookie sheet can save you from such baking embarrassment and waste. An insulated cookie sheet is typically made of two layers of aluminum with an air pocket in between that helps prevent uneven baking and burnt bottoms. Another option, for a bit more money, is a rectangular baking stone, which will help ensure evenly baked cookies every time.

❈ If the butter begins to melt as you're creaming butter and sugar, pop the batter, bowl, and beaters into the fridge for 10 to 15 minutes, then take them out and continue creaming.

❈ To slowly add dry ingredients when your mixer is running, create a temporary tool to get the ingredients into the rotating bowl—and not all over the counter—while protecting your fingers from the beaters. Take a sheet of waxed paper, fold it in half lengthwise, and crease it on the fold. Open the paper and lay it, crease down, on the counter. Pour your dry ingredients into the crease. Bring the long sides of the paper back together, and hold them between the fingers of one hand. With the other hand, support the paper from underneath as you lift it. Put one end of this makeshift trough just inside the mixing bowl, and lift the opposite end so the ingredients flow directly into the bowl.

❋ Your cookies will bake more evenly if the dollops of dough are the same size when you put them in the oven. A quick and easy way to accomplish this is to use a small ice cream scoop to dole out the dough.

❋ To make the flakiest piecrusts, always use lard—there simply is no other fat that will produce the same mouthwatering results.

❋ Before putting a pan of cake batter in the oven to bake, tap the cake pan on the counter to bring any air bubbles to the surface; it will keep the inside of your cake from resembling Swiss cheese.

❋ To keep fruit from turning to mush in your fruit cobblers, begin with frozen fruit. The fruit will thaw during baking without getting overcooked.

❋ To properly measure flour, spoon the flour into the measuring cup and level it off with the straight edge of a knife. Do not tap the measuring cup to settle the flour as you fill it, do not use the measuring cup to scoop flour straight from the container, and do not pack the flour into the cup; otherwise, you'll end up adding too much flour, which can result in baked goods that are dense and heavy rather than light and fluffy.

❋ Always take the time to preheat your oven.

❋ Know how your oven bakes. All ovens have hot spots and cooler spots, and some ovens bake hotter and quicker than others. Don't be afraid to adjust a recipe's specified baking time and/or temperature to suit your oven's peculiarities.

❋ Keep your oven door closed, or you'll risk a fallen cake or under-done pie. If you have an oven light, use it to peek at your goodies, but don't leave it on during baking.

❋ When making cookies, cakes, and pies, it's best to sift the dry ingredients together unless the recipe directs otherwise. If you don't have a sifter, use a fork to gently but thoroughly combine the dry ingredients.

❋ To remove a stubbornly stuck cake from a pan, set the warm pan on a wet cloth for five minutes. The wet cloth will create a steaming action in the pan that will release the cake.

❋ Break eggs into a separate bowl to avoid getting any shell pieces in your dessert.

❋ When beating egg whites, be sure the eggs are at room temperature and the bowl is clean—even a tiny bit of yolk, oil, or water can keep the eggs from getting stiff.

❋ If you are separating egg whites and get some yolk in the mix, use a paper towel to dab at and remove the bits of yolk from the whites.

MAKE KITCHEN CLEANUP A BREEZE

Decades ago, cleaning the kitchen meant hours of scrubbing and scouring. Few cooks in this day and age would forgo all of the modern tools and products that have made that chore easier and less time-consuming. But heartland cooks know that many of the kitchen-cleaning tricks that have been passed down to them still work as well or better than anything currently on the market—and usually without using toxic chemicals. We've collected a variety of their time-tested tips and strategies in this chapter, so you can give them a go in your own kitchen.

Pamper Your Appliances

**Now, as always, the most automated appliance
in a household is the mother.**

—BEVERLY JONES

Keeping kitchen appliances clean and well maintained is key not only to extending their lives but to getting the best from them, which can save you money. Fortunately, you don't need to purchase expensive chemical cleaners to keep your appliances free of grease, mold, sticky residue, bits of food, and other gunk. Simple, traditional heartland cleaning solutions and tips will generally do the trick.

❋ To make cleaning the burner grates from a gas stovetop easier, first soak them in hot water to which you've added a dash of dishwashing liquid. After a five- to ten-minute soak, use a soft brush to scrub away all the burnt-on food remnants. Use the same method to clean electric burner coils.

Thank Thomas

Although various versions of the mop have been around for a long time, the first modern mop was reportedly invented by Thomas Stewart. Stewart received a patent for his innovative mop in 1893. What made his mop unique? You could wring it out by simply moving a lever on the mop handle rather than having to bend over and wring out the mop head by hand.

❋ It's also much easier to remove stuck-on food from burner pans if they are first soaked in hot, soapy water. But if the pans still feel greasy, wipe them down with a soft cloth or paper towel saturated with white vinegar, or try soaking them a second time in a mixture of white vinegar and water, then wipe them dry.

❋ To clean burnt food particles from the burner of your stove, sprinkle it with a small amount of salt, then immediately wipe it away. An extra heartland trick: Add a little ground cinnamon to the salt that you sprinkle on the burner; a lovely apple-pie aroma will waft from the burner and fill your kitchen with a home-sweet-home scent the next time you turn it on.

❋ To remove baked-on spills from your oven floor, use a little patience instead of lots of caustic chemicals: First, brush away any large bits of burnt food using an old toothbrush. Then soak a rag or paper towel with water, and lay it on the spill (cover multiple spills if they're close enough to one another). Flatten the sopping-wet cloth against the crusty or sticky area, leave it in place for 30 minutes or so, and then simply wipe away the gunk with the rag or paper towel. Repeat the soaking process as necessary to get rid of any stuck-on bits that remain.

❋ If the inside of your oven needs a more thorough cleaning, try this: Fill an aluminum pan halfway with ammonia, and carefully slide the pan into your cool oven. Close the door, and let the ammonia work its magic overnight. The next day, pull out the pan of ammonia and carefully pour the liquid, along with an equal amount of water, into a cleaning bucket. (Be sure the kitchen is well-ventilated when you do this.) Wearing rubber gloves, dampen a rag with the ammonia solution, and wipe down the oven's inner surfaces and racks.

Borrow from the Bathroom

Some common bathroom supplies can actually make cleaning your kitchen surfaces and tools easier.

• To deep-clean a porcelain sink, fill it with warm water and put in two or three denture-cleaning tablets. Let them work for five minutes, then drain and wipe down the sink with a damp cloth.

• Use dental floss and an old toothbrush to remove dirt caught in all the hard-to-reach crevices of your kitchen faucet, and use cotton swabs to clean around the fixture.

• Toothbrushes are great for getting the gunk out of kitchen gadgets such as can openers, garlic presses, strainers, and graters.

❋ The best way to avoid the need for caustic oven cleaners is to catch spills before they hit the oven floor. So once you've cleaned your oven using the preceding tips, try this trick to protect it: When baking a dish that could bubble over or spill, fill a larger-size baking pan (a disposable aluminum one will do) with a quarter to a half inch of water, and place it on the rack or oven floor below the food you're baking. The larger pan will catch spills before they reach the oven floor, and the layer of water will prevent any spilled food from burning, which will keep that unpleasant burnt-food aroma from taking over your kitchen.

❋ Newer electric stovetops and microwaves have touch pads that can be very sensitive to harsh cleaning products and even water. To clean these newfangled control panels, turn to that old heartland standby—white vinegar. Lightly moisten a soft cloth with the vinegar, and wipe down the touch pads and the rest of the stovetop or microwave to remove greasy fingerprints and other gunky buildup.

❋ Use white vinegar to clean and maintain the door seal of your refrigerator, too. A regular wipe down with a vinegar-moistened cloth (and perhaps some cotton-tipped swabs or an old toothbrush dipped in vinegar as well) will remove food crumbs and spills and prevent mold from taking hold.

❋ If your fridge begins to smell a bit stale, use dry coffee grounds or whole coffee beans to freshen it. Place the beans or dry grounds (to dry the grounds after brewing, spread them in a thin layer on a cookie sheet or piece of aluminum foil) in a small jar or can, and cover the opening with a piece of cheesecloth held in place with a rubber band. The coffee will quickly do away with the musty smell. To keep unpleasant odors from overwhelming your refrigerator in the future, replace the dry grounds every few weeks, or put an open box of baking soda on an icebox shelf and replace it every few months.

> ## Handy Hint
>
> Vacuum behind and underneath your refrigerator at least once a month to prevent dust from building up on condenser coils. Your icebox will need to work harder—and use more energy—to keep your perishables cold if the coils are dusty.

✳ To clean and deodorize the inside surfaces and shelves of your icebox, wet a clean sponge with a solution of baking soda and water, and wipe them down.

✳ To get rid of fingerprints on stainless-steel appliances, put a tiny amount of baby oil on a soft cloth or paper towel and rub the fingerprints away.

✳ You may feel like giving up on ever removing that stubborn layer of grease from the outside of the stove, rangetop, and range hood, but don't throw in the towel just yet. You can conquer it! First, try scrubbing in a circular motion with a dish rag soaked in a mixture of hot water and dishwashing liquid. (You'll probably need to put some muscle behind it in order to start shifting that sticky coating.) If that doesn't do the trick, reach for that kitchen-cleaning staple—white vinegar. Fill a clean spray bottle with the vinegar, and spray it directly on the greasy surfaces. Wait about five minutes, then scrub with a rag or thick paper towels soaked in hot water.

✳ Ironic as it may sound, another heartland secret for getting rid of a coating of sticky grease from the outside of a stove or other appliance is to fight fire with fire—or, more precisely, to fight grease with grease. Pour a bit of cooking oil onto a rag or sturdy paper towel, rub the grease-covered appliance with it, and watch that sticky film come off. Then wash down the surface with a clean rag or sponge dipped frequently in a solution of hot water and dishwashing liquid.

✳ To clean your automatic drip coffeemaker, put a denture-cleaning tablet in the water-storage compartment, pour in hot water, then run the brew cycle. After the denture-tablet bath, run the brew cycle a couple more times with plain water before making coffee again.

✳ Is the inside surface of your coffeemaker's glass carafe so clouded with mineral scale or coffee stains that you can't see through it? Or, even worse, is the bottom of the carafe covered in burnt coffee because someone forgot to turn the coffeemaker off? Don't worry. You can save it with this simple recipe: First, be sure the carafe has cooled to room temperature. Then, pour in 4 teaspoons salt, 1 tablespoon water, and 1 cup crushed ice. Gently swirl the mixture in the carafe until the glass is once again clear. (If the liquid gets so gunky that you can't tell if the glass is clean, dump it out; if necessary, make a fresh batch and swirl some more.) Then pour the mixture out, rinse the carafe, and wash as usual.

❄ To clean and freshen your dish-washer and help dissolve hard-water stains, fill the detergent cup with unsweetened powdered lemonade, and run the empty dishwasher through its regular cycle. (A mild acid that's naturally found in lemons and lemonade helps to dislodge stuck-on food particles and crusty water stains.)

> **Handy Hint**
>
> Next time you load the dishwasher, include the kitchen-sink strainer and oven knobs (put them on the top rack), your dish rag (hang it on the top rack), and your fridge drawers (bottom rack).

❄ To clean and deodorize your microwave, fill a coffee mug with water and either two or three slices of fresh lemon or a few tablespoons of lemon juice, place it in the microwave, and run the appliance on high for three minutes. When the cycle has ended, let the mug sit for a few more minutes, then remove it and discard the lemons and water. Any caked-on food or grease can then be easily wiped away with a clean cloth or paper towel.

❄ If your garbage disposal seems a bit sluggish and smelly, run a combination of ice cubes and orange, lemon, or lime peels through it. The citrus peels will help flush away malodorous residue, and the ice will help sharpen the blades.

❄ To loosen hard-water stains from your kitchen faucet, cut a lemon in half and rub the juicy flesh over the encrusted mineral deposits. Then use a soft scrubber to rub away the stains. (You can make a perfectly good scrubber by balling up an old clean athletic sock and covering it with the foot section of a clean nylon knee-high or footie stocking.) If any stains remain, squeeze juice from the lemon onto the stubborn deposits, let it sit for 30 to 60 minutes, then scrub again.

Make Dishwashing Less Demanding

Thank God for dirty dishes
They have a tale to tell;
While others may go hungry,
We're eating very well.

—AUTHOR UNKNOWN

These heartland tips can take some of the toil out of cleaning dishes, utensils, pots, and pans.

* Trying to get dried-on egg residue off pans and plates can be a real chore. To keep the egg remnants from sticking like glue in the first place, sprinkle salt on them as soon as you're finished with the pan or plate. The salt will absorb the moisture that would otherwise cause the eggs to harden on the plate, making it easy to wipe the egg away.

* Remove stains on plastic or rubber utensils by gently scrubbing them with a sponge or washcloth dabbed in a paste of baking soda and water.

✳ To remove stains from plastic food-storage containers, reach for some dental hygiene products. Say you have a container that's stained reddish-orange after holding tomato sauce. Fill the container with hot water, and drop in two denture-cleaning tablets. Let the tablets work for about 5 to 10 minutes, then pour out the solution and wash as usual. If some staining still remains, get out a toothbrush, wet it with warm water, and either dab it in a handful of baking soda or squeeze some tooth-paste (it has to be the paste variety, not the gel) onto it. Then scrub away at the remaining stains, rinse, and wash as usual.

✳ To remove a strong food odor from a plastic food-storage container, combine warm water, 3 to 5 drops of dishwashing liquid, and a quarter cup white vinegar in the container. Cover the container tightly, and shake. Leave the mixture in the container overnight, then dump it out and wash and rinse the container the next day.

After Raw Meat, Soap and Heat

Cleaning up properly during and after food preparation is more than a matter of aesthetics. It's essential for preventing certain foodborne illnesses. And never is that more true than when you have been work-ing with raw meat, poultry, or fish. Everything—every utensil, every tool, every surface, and every hand—that has come in contact with raw meat or its juices should be washed thoroughly in hot, soapy water before it is allowed to touch or hold anything else. The same goes for anything that touches raw poultry, raw fish, or their respective juices.

Cleaning Cast Iron

Seasoning a cast-iron skillet (as described on pages 20–21) gives the pan a nonstick surface. To maintain that nonstick surface, you can't clean the pan the way you would other cookware. You can't soak it in water or use dishwashing liquid or other detergent. Instead, right after you finish cooking, wipe out the pan with a paper towel (or a rag you use only for cast iron) or rinse it in hot water and immediately dry it with paper towels (otherwise rust can form on the pan). Then use a paper towel to apply a light coating of cooking oil, and stow it. (If dust tends to settle on the pan between uses, keep it lightly covered with a small kitchen towel.)

✱ If there is scorched food stuck to the bottom of a pot or pan, fill the cookware with water and add a denture-cleaning tablet or two; the denture cleaner will help lift food off the pot or pan the same way it lifts tiny food particles and stains off artificial choppers.

✱ If you don't have a denture tablet handy, another easy way to get scorched food off cookware is to cover the bottom of the pot or pan with baking soda, add water, and boil the mixture for about ten minutes. Most of the burnt-on mess should float right out when you drain the water, and any remnants should be soft enough to be wiped away with a paper towel.

✱ To restore the shine to aluminum pots and pans, fill them with water, add apple peels, and boil. To maintain that shine from day to day, wipe them with a paper towel moistened with lemon juice after washing them.

❋ Get greasy residue off glassware by adding a small amount of ammonia to your dishwater. (Whenever you use ammonia, work in a well-ventilated area and wear a pair of rubber or vinyl household gloves to protect your hands.)

❋ Allow cookie sheets and baking pans to cool down completely before you wash them. Cleaning them while they're still hot may warp them.

❋ To remove brown spots from glass bakeware, mix baking soda and water into a paste, dab an old toothbrush into the paste, and use the toothbrush to scrub away the spots. Then wash the bakeware as usual. Try this same trick to get rid of brown spots on the inside of your oven window (unless the manufacturer's directions advise otherwise), then finish up by wiping the paste off the window with a damp cloth or paper towel.

❋ Don't soak stainless-steel and silver utensils together. The silver will turn black during the soak.

❋ If silver utensils get tarnished, spread them on an aluminum cookie sheet, sprinkle with baking soda, drizzle hot water over them, and use a soft cloth to rub the wet baking soda over each one. Rinse, and dry thoroughly before storing.

❋ Moisture can damage silver, so when storing silverware, place a piece of sidewalk chalk in the drawer to absorb moisture.

CREATE A COZY HEARTLAND KITCHEN

The kitchen has always been the heart of the heartland home. Nothing can compare to a good meal and good conversation shared around the kitchen table. It's a place where memories are made and laughter lingers. In this chapter, you'll find simple, inexpensive suggestions for creating the kind of cozy, comfortable space that invites folks to sit, eat, talk—and stay awhile.

Take Care of the Clutter

**If you can organize your kitchen,
you can organize your life.**

—LOUIS PARRISH

A disorganized kitchen creates an atmosphere that is more chaotic than comfortable. So the first step in crafting a welcoming kitchen is to declutter. Use these tips to keep your stuff from overwhelming your space.

❋ Safety pins, broken crayons, candles, single batteries, hair scrunchies, scissors, lost buttons, the odd screwdriver, spare keys, receipts—these are just a few of the odds and ends that seem to migrate to the kitchen junk drawer (and the counter, and the table). Instead of complaining about the mess, organize it. First, toss out the broken pens and bottle caps, and return things that belong in other rooms. Then, use the tops and bottoms of small boxes, shallow plastic baskets and small plastic bins, or inexpensive drawer dividers to organize the items you really want to keep in the kitchen drawers.

❄ Homey heartland kitchens are known for their assortment of colorful doodads and knickknacks—pretty or kitschy things displayed for fun, interest, or sentimental reasons. They add character and can be great conversation starters. But too many can overwhelm the kitchen and get in the way of everyday tasks (not to mention that someone—like you—has to dust them all regularly). If you can't relocate or part with enough of them, consider displaying smaller groupings of related ones on a rotating basis (seasonally, perhaps).

Bountiful Baskets

Woven baskets are a hallmark of heartland kitchens, calling forth images of Laura Ingalls running through the fields with a bounty of fresh-picked berries or of Aunt Bee taking lunch to Andy and Barney at the station. To instantly give your kitchen a more homey feel, consider making liberal use of these practical decorations. Hang a collection from your ceiling or display them on top of your cabinets so they're close at hand when you need them. Use one to hold ripe fruit or a loose bouquet of freshly cut flowers from your garden. Corral often-used utensils in another basket, and pull it out when it's time to set the table. Place a smaller basket on the counter to hold napkins. The possibilities are endless.

✳ Get the best of both worlds by using practical decorations in your heartland kitchen. For example, don't just display your collection of old tins from bygone days—put them to work! Turn them into attractive places to store things you need in the kitchen, such as recipe cards, cookie cutters, paper cupcake liners, matchbooks, snack-bag clips, coasters—you get the picture.

✳ If smaller kitchen gadgets and tools become jumbled in a drawer, give them order by storing them in paper-towel rolls. Use tape to cover one end of each cardboard roll, label each with the name of the tool stored inside, and lay the rolls side-by-side in one or two layers in the drawer. You'll be able to quickly grab what you need without wrestling with a pile of tangled tools.

✳ Designate a decorative country basket or a clean, old-fashioned, rectangular cookie tin as a sort of drop box for mail, sale fliers, catalogs, school permission slips, health-care receipts, and other everyday paper items that would otherwise end up cluttering your countertop or table. Remind every member of the household that such items should go directly into the basket or tin. Then, at the end of the day, take a few minutes to go through the papers, and file, throw out, or otherwise "process" each piece.

✳ Use the inner surface of cupboard and closet doors to keep oft-used items out of sight. Buy plastic hooks with adhesive backing that won't damage the doors when you remove them. Or try this trick: With a glue gun, attach one magnet to a pincher-style clothespin and another magnet to the inside of a cabinet door to create a detachable hanger for rubber gloves, oven mitts, kitchen towels, and other lightweight items.

✸ Don't overlook the underside of upper cabinets. See if you can clear more counter or table space by attaching small appliances (such as the electric can opener or coffeemaker), a paper-towel holder, or other countertop residents to the bottom surface of the cabinets above your kitchen counters.

Create Your Own Heartland Style

**A house that does not have one worn,
comfy chair in it is soulless.**

—MAY SARTON

Creating a functional yet inviting heartland kitchen that reflects your personality can be easier and more affordable than you'd think. Consider the following suggestions.

✸ Use color to tie the room together. Survey your kitchen furniture, appliances, drapes, tablecloths, and even knickknacks to pick out a color for the walls that feels warm and inviting to you and will go with your appliances and/or furniture (unless you plan on replacing them at the same time). Paint one or more walls the chosen color, maybe add a tablecloth or placements in the same hue, and watch the whole room start to come together.

New Places for Old Placemats

Instead of throwing away your old kitchen placemats, put them to a new use. Quilted placemats work great as impromptu potholders, while cloth or vinyl placemats are great for lining the bottom of utensil drawers, cabinets, or picnic baskets. If you sew, you can get really creative. For example, you could fold an old quilted placemat in half widthwise and sew the short ends closed to create a cushioned storage pocket to protect packed shoes when you travel. Or you could stitch together the two long edges of a cloth placemat and sew elastic into the ends to create a plastic-bag holder/dispenser that's just as good as the kind sold for several dollars in grocery stores.

✳ Take a fresh look at your room. Pretend you're a first-time guest in your kitchen. Sit in every seat at the table, and check out the view from each one. Focus on what your family members or friends actually see when they are sitting in each seat: Are they staring at a blank wall or an overcrowded, disorganized countertop? Do they have a lovely view of the garbage cans in back as they gaze out through the kitchen window? Make simple changes—hang an interesting piece of artwork or a collection of photos on the blank wall, clear the clutter off the counter and replace it with a set of quaint kitchen canisters, move the garbage cans to a different spot— to ensure that those who share your table are treated to a pleasing view.

✳ Use inexpensive, direct-from-nature decorations to add simple beauty and rustic charm to your kitchen. Scan your yard or nearby woods for ideas. A basket of pine cones, a bunch of dried herbs or pussy willows tied together with a pretty ribbon, a vase of fresh-cut flowers from the yard, a bowl of acorns, or even a plate of colorful stones can add an under-stated natural touch to your kitchen table or counter.

✳ Along the same natural lines, consider growing some herbs in pretty, color-ful pots on your kitchen windowsill. It's a handy and attractive way to bring the outside in and put fresh herbs right at your fingertips when you're cooking.

Handy Hint

Flea markets, thrift stores, and yard or garage sales are great places to dig up used-but-unique treasures for decorating your kitchen and other rooms in your home. While it can be fun to shop antique stores, their prices can be a bit steep. Though it may take a bit of elbow grease to clean or refurbish a thrift-store find, you'll be glad you made the effort when you add that perfect touch of real heartland history to your kitchen décor.

✳ Use a couple of washable throw rugs to warm up the kitchen—both figuratively and literally. Add nonslip backing to each so you don't end up going for an inadvertent and potentially haz-ardous ride on one of them.

✳ Remember that everything doesn't have to match. True heartland, or country, kitchens tend to have a laid-back, lived-in, patchwork charm, like that of a favorite hand-me-down quilt. So feel free to find things you love and bring them together. Functional, frugal, clean, cozy, inviting—those are words to focus on when creating your heartland kitchen. It's an approach used in countless heartland kitchens and throughout many a heartland home, and it's one that makes decorating easier on you and your wallet.

✳ Be practical, creative, and thrifty. Suspend an old wooden ladder over your kitchen island or counter, and use it as a pot hanger. Polish up an old armoire and turn it into a silver or linen cupboard. Cover a tired-looking shelf with a little paint and a lacy runner, and top it with a display of pretty heirloom plates. Turn a collection of old, weathered kitchen utensils from the thrift store or your great-aunt's attic into decorations for your kitchen wall. Use your imagination to find new uses for old treasures—it's a prized tradition in the heartland!

Every house where love abides
And friendship is a guest,
Is surely home, and home sweet home
For there the heart can rest.

—HENRY VAN DYKE